WHY DUCKS
DO THAT

Why Ducks Do That

40 Distinctive Duck Behaviors Explained & Photographed

by Chuck Petrie

Willow Creek Press

Published by Willow Creek Press
P.O. Box 147, Minocqua, Wisconsin 54548

Editor: Andrea K. Donner

Photo Credits: p.2 © BillMarchel.com; p.8 © robertmccaw.com; p.10 © Cathy & Gordon Illg; p.12 © John R. Ford; p.14-15 © S. J. Krasemann/Peter Arnold, Inc.; p.16 © robertmccaw.com; p.18-19 © Steve & Dave Maslowski; p.20 © John R. Ford; p.22 © Carl R. Sams II/Peter Arnold, Inc.; p.24 © robertmccaw.com; p.26, 28 © BillMarchel.com; p.30, 32 © robertmccaw.com; p.34-35 © Tom Vezo/Peter Arnold, Inc.; p.36, 38 © robertmccaw.com; p.40 © S. Nielsen/ UNEP/Peter Arnold, Inc.; p.42 © Carl R. Sams II/Peter Arnold, Inc.; p.44 © John R. Ford; p.46 © Steve & Dave Maslowski; p.48 © robertmccaw.com; p.50 © Steve & Dave Maslowski; p.52 © John R. Ford; p.54 © robertmccaw.com; p.56 © BillMarchel.com; p.58, 60 © Cathy & Gordon Illg; p.62 © Steve & Dave Maslowski; p.64 © www.garykramer.net; p.66,68 © BillMarchel.com; p.70 © Cathy & Gordon Illg; p.72 © robertmccaw.com; p.74 © www.garykramer.net; p.76 © BillMarchel.com; p.78 © robertmccaw.com; p.82 © BillMarchel.com; p.84 © robertmccaw.com; p.86-87 © Tom Vezo/Peter Arnold, Inc.; p.88, 90 © BillMarchel.com; p.92 © robertmccaw.com; p.94 © Steve & Dave Maslowski; p.96 © robertmccaw.com

Library of Congress Cataloging-in-Publication Data

Petrie, Chuck.
   Why ducks do that : 40 distinctive waterfowl behaviors / explained & photographed by Chuck Petrie.
      p. cm.
   ISBN 1-59543-050-4 (hardcover : alk. paper)
   1. Ducks--Behavior.   2. Ducks--Behavior--Pictorial works.   I. Title.
QL696.A52P42 2006
598.4'115--dc22

                                                        2006007570

Printed in Canada

Table of Contents

The Lesser Scaup is popularly called a "bluebill." Although its vocalizations are rarely heard, it emits guttural scolding notes and sharp whistles.

Why do ducks make so many different sounds?

Interpreting the wide assortment of whistles, grunts, quacks, coos, clucks, and trills made by various species of ducks is difficult. But all of these vocalizations, which are considered calls rather than songs, are instinctive in nature, and all serve the purpose of communicating information.

Communication between members of a species is critical to survival (alerting others to the presence of a predator, for example), is necessary to attract and identify mates, and is used to encourage socialization, among other important functions. Each species has its own vocal repertoire (although closely related species' vocalizations may sound similar), and because of physical dissimilarities in their "voice boxes," adult males and females of the same species have distinctively different calls.

Ducks begin to hear their species' specific language before they even hatch. In the late stages of incubation, a hen duck will make low-volume vocalizations while on her nest. Forty-eight hours prior to hatching, during their pipping stage of development, ducklings are capable of hearing these maternal calls and also begin making their own vocalizations. This communication between unhatched siblings helps synchronize their hatching and also helps them to identify the voices of their brothers and sisters; hearing the maternal calls of the hen helps the ducklings identify their mother by her voice and also facilitates their imprinting on her. In the days after hatching, vocalizations between the hen and ducklings will allow them to keep in contact with one another when they feed in thick vegetation, and the hen will use specific calls to notify her offspring of the presence of predators.

As adults, ducks instinctively begin using their voices to attract mates. In mallards, for example, courting drakes perform physical displays and emit a grunt-whistle vocalization to prospective mates; if a hen is receptive to that male, she will answer with a receptive posture and what is termed an *incitement call*. As well as helping them learn to identify each other by their voices, this calling helps to reinforce the mates' pair bond relationship.

These Redhead ducklings could walk, swim, and eat on their own just hours after hatching.

Why do mother ducks feed their young differently than songbirds?

Ducks—like upland birds such as pheasants—are what biologists term *nidifugous* birds, which means they leave the nest soon after hatching. Conversely, songbird species are termed *nidicolous,* which means they are reared for a time in the nest. Nidicolous species are hatched almost naked, with only small amounts of downy feathering to keep them warm, and are essentially helpless, unable to walk or feed themselves. Therefore, songbird mothers (and in many cases fathers too) must sit on their nestlings after they hatch in order to keep them warm, and the parents must bring food to their young at least until (and sometimes after) the young birds grow feathers and can fly and forage for food on their own.

Both nidifugous and nidicolous birds are born with a yolk sack (absorbed into their abdomen during egg development) to provide them with an initial source of nourishment. But because ducklings are not fed by their mother (and their father is long gone), once they hatch they must begin to obtain additional nourishment before their nutrient reserves are used up. Nidifugous birds are born covered with natal down and are capable of walking. The energy reserve supplied by their yolk sack provides ducklings with sustenance during their first journey when, immediately after hatching, their mother leads them from the nest to a wetland where they can feed themselves. For ground-nesting birds such as ducks, leaving the nest soon after hatching is imperative, as ducklings are extremely vulnerable to predators while still in the nest. Also, during the later stages of incubation, the hen will have eaten little and will have lost as much as a quarter of her body mass. Her survival and that of her brood requires a quick exodus from the nest site in order to find food, water, and protective brood cover.

When ducklings begin feeding, their diet is almost exclusively composed of insects and small aquatic invertebrates. Later, when they grow older, the ducklings' diet will expand to include aquatic seeds and tubers as well as grains, acorns, and other food items.

The Canvasback is one of the largest North American diving ducks. In contrast to talkative dabbling ducks, the "Can" and other divers are more subdued in their vocalization.

Why do diving ducks and dabbling ducks make such different calls?

Diving ducks do make vocalizations (calls), but they are barely audible to the human ear, as are some dabbler drake calls. Diving duck males are also generally less vocal than dabbling duck males during courtship. Their display calls are usually subdued mewing, whirring, or cooing notes. The male redhead, the most demonstrative of the "macho" divers, renders a preposterous *me-ow*, similar to the vocalization of a cat. Drake sea ducks are more effusive than divers when vocalizing their expressions of love: Common eider males issue soothing yet relatively loud cooing noises to mates; the drake oldsquaw, perhaps the most expressive of drakes in his terms of endearment, bellows a wild, almost maniacal yodeling call that can be heard for half a mile.

Not all calls made by drakes to their mates or prospective mates are strictly linked to ritualized mating displays. Some are "conversational" in nature and issued while in flight or on the water. The drake wigeon (a dabbler), for example, frequently calls to its mate while in flight, issuing a piping, three-note whistle, the middle note higher than the others. While on the wing, too, the pintail (also a dabbler) drake serenades its mate with distinctive flutelike whistle notes. Mallard drakes soothe their hens with a raspy, low-volume *reeeb-reeeb* call.

Female diving ducks are considerably less vocal than their female counterparts among dabbling ducks. Most diver hens issue a harsh, growl-like trilling call and lack the "quacking" notes typical of female dabblers. When accompanied by their mate and spurning overtures of other amorous males, hen divers and dabblers both issue an "incitement call," which serves to thwart unsolicited male advances and direct aggression from their mate toward the unwanted suitors. When not with their mate or when not sexually receptive at all, the hens of both classes may direct a "repulsion call," similar to the incitement call, toward romantically inclined drakes.

Probably no species of duck has been extensively studied, as far as its language is concerned, as the wood duck. Although the male woody's finchlike *twee, twee* call is barely audible, the hen is especially known for a screaming *wee-e-e-k, wee-e-e-k* call. This drawn-out, owl-like call serves more than one purpose, depending on its intensity and the context in which it is broadcast: It can serve as a warning call, or it can be used in social situations. Female wood ducks also vent other call notes, including a "go away" note, a danger call, a general call note, brood call notes, and a mate-attracting "coquette" call, among others. (The parallels with human infatuation-speak are ominous—the girls are outspoken yet coquettish in their love talk; the males bumble through courtship with murmured burps, wheezes, and whistles.) Ah! The call of the wild.

Mallards are known as "surface feeding" ducks because they dip and dabble in the shallows, and usually do not dive. They are perhaps the most vocally communicative of all North American ducks and use a number of calls for conversation and courtship.

This Mallard drake and hen are resting on a log in a typical small wetland that provides high concentrations of invertebrates and crustaceans.

Why do ducks prefer to inhabit small, shallow wetlands during spring migration?

Small wetlands warm faster than large bodies of water, providing migrating waterfowl a veritable duck soup (actually, more of a primordial *soup du jour* of food items called invertebrates). Those tiny creatures are a diverse lot and include insects and their larvae (flies, midges, mosquitoes, beetles, mayflies and such); crustaceans such as tiny clams; water fleas; scuds (several species of freshwater shrimp); dozens of species of snails, plus may other minute animals. And while you wouldn't want to see these squishy, wiggling life forms in a glass of drinking water, they play an irreplaceable role in ducks' diets and reproductive cycles.

Invertebrates are ducks' major sources of protein. Protein contains amino acids—in essence, the ducks' essential vitamins—necessary to synthesize enzymes and hormones, to build and replace body tissues and feathers, and to produce eggs. Comparing protein content on a percentage basis of invertebrates to that contained in natural aquatic plant foods or agricultural foods such as corn

or wheat, invertebrates supply several times the measure, and they are much more easily digested.

Invertebrates are further crucial to ducks because they comprise almost 100 percent of ducklings' diets during their first weeks of life, when most food is converted to tissue growth. Invertebrates, especially snails and tiny clams, are also primary sources of calcium, which female ducks require to form eggshells.

Because of hens' increased requirements of protein at certain times of the year, especially in spring when they are laying eggs, invertebrates may make up as much as 76 percent of female dabbling ducks' diets and 90 percent of female pochards' (canvasback and redhead) diets. Fortunately for these breeding hens, and a short while later for their ducklings, protein-rich invertebrates reach peak abundance in early to late spring in shallow, flooded wetlands. During this critical period, these temporary soup kitchens not only abound with invertebrate life but, because they are shallow, provide fertile foraging grounds for breeding hens and their ducklings. The shallow water of the wetlands presents invertebrates in high densities where ducks can easily feed at or near the surface, without having to dive for food, which requires large expenditures of valuable energy.

Whereas geese obtain most of their protein from plant matter (their primary food) and can satisfy their intake requirements on breeding grounds by consuming sedges and grasses, ducks are not so fortunate. Neither can ducks "transport" protein reserves from wintering grounds to breeding ground. Protein, unlike fat, can't be stored in large quantities nor, like carbohydrates (sugars, starches, celluloses derived from plant foods), can it be easily converted to fat.

Thus the importance of hens finding and consuming large quantities of invertebrates on their breeding grounds in spring is critical to their reproductive success.

A mated pair of wood ducks cruise a small pond. The hen, who will nest nearby, requires a protein rich diet during egg laying. The pond with its high density of invertebrates provides quick and easy access to this necessary food.

Wood Ducks usually build their nests in a natural hollow of a trunk or cavity in a large branch of a tree. They can nest in the hollow of a tree a mile or more from water.

Why do some ducks nest in trees?

For some species of ducks, nesting in a tree cavity is the ultimate solution to their housing problems. Be it a natural tree cavity or an artificial nesting box, more than 18 species of ducks worldwide, including 11 native to North America, prefer to live in a room with a view for the nesting season.

Hens of the tree-nesting species prefer setting up their nurseries in elevated housing primarily for security purposes. That is, ducks that nest in tree cavities or nesting boxes versus other nesting sites—such as on the ground in upland sites (e.g., mallards) or in emergent vegetation over water (e.g., canvasback)—generally lose fewer eggs to nest predators. Tree-nesting hens still see the proverbial wolf at the door, including, in North America, the ubiquitous and always-hungry raccoon, egg-eating rat and bull snakes, red and fox squirrels, and omelet-loving songbirds, especially starlings. But tree nesters still enjoy greater success when it comes to hatching their clutches.

Tree-nesting ducks are native to Indonesia, South and Central America, Asia, Australia, Europe, Eurasia, Africa, and North America. Most of these birds belong to a tribe of waterfowl known as perching ducks; the rest are sea ducks, whistling ducks and a few species of dabbling ducks. Stamped in recent decades, however, the most familiar duck among this tribe is the too-good-for-its-looks wood duck.

Of the whistling ducks, nine species of this long-legged tribe are found around the globe. In the United States, the black-bellied whistling duck is found primarily in southern Texas and southern Arizona. (Most nest in cavities in oak, ebony, hackberry, and mesquite trees, but some will build ground nests, especially where they can't find suitable, or any, trees.) The fulvous whistling duck is found from the Texas coast to Louisiana and southern Florida (some also reside in southern California).

Other tree-nesting sea ducks in North America include the wood duck, the harlequin (which more commonly nests in snags and rocky crevices along streams), the common goldeneye, the Barrow's goldeneye, the bufflehead, and the common and hooded mergansers.

These are Wood Duck eggs in the nest. Some wood duck hens lay eggs in neighboring nests and abandon the incubation and brood rearing chores altogether.

Why do some ducks lay eggs in other ducks' nests?

Some ducks make rotten mothers. They've no compunctions about abandoning their young, much less nurturing them, and if it weren't for an obscure form of animal foster care, the offspring of these hens would receive no guardianship at all. These ducks leave their eggs furtively deposited in the nests of other birds.

The behavior is called "brood parasitism," or "nest parasitism," and the duck, goose, and swan family *(Anatidae)* is not above the practice. Of 71 bird families worldwide, only five, including the waterfowl family, are known to practice nest parasitism. The phenomenon is relatively uncommon among dabbling ducks, but relatively common among diving ducks and in sea ducks that nest in tree cavities.

Almost all species of duck, geese, and swan are known, on occasion, to lay eggs in the nests of other waterfowl. In most species, however, this conduct does not begin to resemble the degree or frequency of brood parasitism demonstrated by redheads and wood ducks.

Many redhead and wood duck hens build their own nests, incubate their own eggs (and sometimes those of other ducks that have been left in their care), and raise their young to be normal redhead and wood duck ducklings. Some hens of the species do dally in nest parasitism, however, depositing a few eggs here and there before settling down for the season and taking up normal nesting-incubation-house-keeping chores. Still other hens may decide to forgo the motherhood-household scene altogether, leaving all their eggs in foster care in one host nest, or in the nests of several host mothers. (In subsequent years, individual hens may swap roles, when the formerly accommodating moms become partial or completely parasitic layers, and vice versa.)

Wood ducks search out other wood ducks' nests for foster homes; redheads aren't quite as selective—they'll leave their eggs with many other duck species, including mallards, lesser scaup, and other redheads, but in some locations they are remarkably partial to canvasback hosts' nests.

All ducks, including this Northern Pintail carry some forms of external and internal parasites. The majority of waterfowl are unaffected and remain healthy despite being parasitized.

Why do some people think wild ducks are full of parasites and refuse to eat them?

Mallophagans (a taxonomic classification for what are commonly know as duck lice)—flat, squiggly critters about a quarter of an inch long—are some of the many parasites that freeload on ducks and geese. Like the proverbial brother-in-law who comes for dinner but stays for a year, parasites, both internal and external, are a fact of life for waterfowl. More than 1,000 species of internal parasitic *(endoparasitic)* worms alone—including roundworms, flukes, tapeworms, and everyone's favorite, thorny-headed worms—have been cataloged as infecting waterfowl. Add to this the external *(ectoparasitic)* forms of mites, ticks, flies, fleas, leeches, lice, and other nasties, and you might consider picking up your next duck with a 10-foot pole. Generally speaking, though, ectoparasites are not injurious to waterfowl. Most mites, fleas, and other creepy crawlers that inhabit waterfowl plumage exist by eating epidermal (skin) material, feather debris, down, and body fluids.

And not to worry: Most waterfowl parasites require specific hosts (not you) and, with rare exceptions, can't or won't physically transfer to humans (at least not for long), and if incidentally ingested along with duck meat, can't harm you. With the rare exception of a Lyme-disease-infected tick jumping from duck to duck hunter, you'll probably never be infected by a duck parasite, much less see one.

Most ducks and geese, even though they may commonly carry two dozen or more species of parasites, aren't affected by this excess baggage either. The majority of waterfowl remain healthy despite being parasitized. Only infrequent, severe parasitic infestations cause outright mortality of waterfowl, and then usually as the result of secondary infections by protozoans. Rarely do parasitic epidemics result in appreciable die-offs of ducks and geese.

If you're feeling itchy after reading this, it may not be all in your mind. Humans are no exception when it comes to hosting a plethora of biological parasites, but that's another story (one you probably don't want to know).

A hybrid shoveler/blue-winged teal.

Why do ducks hybridize with other species of ducks?

Simply speaking, hybrid offspring among ducks are the results of mistakes in identity. Hybridization, the cross-mating of two different species of ducks, is usually thwarted by the ability of hens to recognize drakes of their own species by plumage patterns and colors; by the drakes' courtship displays; and possibly by species-distinguishing vocalizations. Still, mistakes happen.

Hybridism among waterfowl is actually relatively frequent. According to noted waterfowl biologist Paul Johnsgard, "Waterfowl, perhaps more than any other avian family, are capable of an extreme genetic capacity for hybridization. Over 400 kinds of interspecies hybrids have been reported for the waterfowl family alone… Most of these have occurred in captivity, but a surprising number have also been reported in the wild."

The all-time champion in duck miscegenation is the mallard, which, worldwide, has been known to breed with as many as 40 other species of waterfowl (including, in captivity, such genetically dissimilar species as greylag geese). The wood duck, known to have successfully crossbred with as many as 20 other duck species, takes second place in the annals of waterfowl hybridization.

A bizarre result of waterfowl crossbreeding is offspring that show distinct characteristics of both parental species. This is especially evident in male offspring resulting from dabbling duck crosses, mallard x pintail hybrid drakes being prime examples. Such hybrid drakes may show the metallic green head of a mallard drake but possess the light blue bill of the male pintail. One of these hybrids might also show the black, white, and predominately blue wing patch, or speculum, of a mallard, but also have the distinctive long, black tail feathers, or "pins," of the pintail drake. Male hybrids from crosses of other duck species often show similar patchwork characteristics indicating their dissimilar genetic heritage.

Identifying female offspring resulting from hybrid crossings is difficult because of females' drab, mottled brown plumage. The female's speculum may show a mix of the parents' colors, but these subtle differences are difficult to recognize.

The Ring-necked Duck might better be called the "ring-billed duck," as its chestnut neck ring is usually seen only at close range, while the white ring on the bill is a prominent field mark. The duck's eye is flattened and unusually large allowing it to see both distant and close objects in sharp focus with a wide field of vision.

Why do ducks have much keener vision than humans?

Like other birds, ducks have the keenest vision of all vertebrates. Compared to a duck's visual abilities, humans have tunnel vision and a nearsighted, blurred view of the world.

Birds' eyes are similar in construction to ours. They have excellent color vision, and their optic nerves, which carry visual messages to the brain, are similar to our sight-sensory pathways. What a duck or a human "sees," after all, is really a series of continuous images formed in the brain from light exciting photosensitive nerve cells in the eyes. But despite the overall similarities in ducks' and humans' optical equipment, there are also dissimilarities, and the images that form in a duck's brain when it views the same scene a human does is something we cannot deduce.

Ducks' eyes, relative to their body size, are enormous. Outwardly, this would not appear to be true, but removing the skin around a duck's eye reveals a large optical structure occupying a significant part of the head. Together, a mallard's eyes, whose size is deceptively masked by their small lid openings, weigh almost as much as the duck's brain.

Unlike the human eye, which is oval-shaped, a duck's eye is flattened. So structured, the duck's eye is like a super wide-angle lens on a camera, capturing a wide field of vision. This eye shape, along with the eye's large size, allows the duck to see close and distant objects in sharp focus. Thus, with one eye pointed outward on each side of its head, a duck can survey an extremely wide field of view. The one negative to having its eyes positioned on opposite sides of its head, is poor binocular vision.

So what advantage does a duck receive from having large, wide-set eyes and largely monocular, instead of binocular vision? First, when flying at high altitudes, ducks need little depth perception. When on the ground or paddling on the water, where they are most susceptible to predators, their wide-set eyes and sharp monocular vision allow ducks to better detect predators above and around them. When flying in close formation with other ducks, having eyes literally on the sides of their head allows the birds to keep safely spaced, avoiding airborne fender benders and serious midair collisions.

Related to the Blue-winged and Cinnamon Teal, the Northern Shoveler favors broad,
shallow marshes where it can use the comb-like teeth along the edges of its
large bill to strain aquatic animals, plants, and seeds from the water.

Why do ducks have such different types of bills?

A diversity of bill forms has helped shape waterfowl into the distinct groups of ducks (and geese) we know today.

This divergence in "beak fashion" all started about 65 million years ago. The various types of today's waterfowl evolved to survive on different kinds of food, and the long-term affinities of the different waterfowl for their "feeding niches" are responsible for the variations we see in waterfowl bill forms. The differences in body configuration have also evolved depending on what the birds eat: diving ducks (adapted to subsurface feeding); sea ducks (mollusk and crustacean feeders); mergansers (specialized for fish capture); and geese (upland grazers).

While outwardly a simple-looking appendage, a duck or goose bill is rather complex. Like the beaks of other birds, the upper and lower bills (mandibles) of waterfowl are formed by a bony core overlaid by compact layers of epidermal cells. Duckbills are only hardened at the tip, or nail. The nail, located on the upper mandible, is used by diving ducks as a pry bar to loosen mollusks attached to rocks and other bottom strata.

While the nail may be utilized as a crowbar, the softer margins of a duck's bill are more like precision instruments. Supplied with sensitive tactile nerve endings, they afford ducks marvelous sensory discrimination, allowing them to detect seeds, insects, crayfish, tiny clams, and other foodstuffs in mud and dark waters.

The margins of ducks' bills also act as sieves, draining water out of the bill while retaining small food items. *Lamellae*—smooth, corduroy like ridges on the margins of the mandibles—provide the filtering action. All ducks and geese have lamellae on their bills, but the structures are more finely developed on some divers and all puddle ducks.

On some diving duck species, particularly sea ducks that consume considerable amounts of fish and small vertebrates, the lamellae are sharper, tooth-like ridges better adapted for grasping and holding prey than for filtering. This is easily seen in the narrow-billed mergansers, whose sharp, exaggerated lamellae have earned them the name "sawbills."

The Common Goldeneye winters wherever water is open in much of the United States. Males winter farther north than females. Next page: Northern Shoveler walking on snow.

Why do ducks rest for long periods in below-freezing weather on snow-covered ground or roost on frigid ponds? Why don't they just fly to someplace warm?

Well, it's in their blood, so to speak, and also in the feathers and skin. Waterfowl have evolved physical and metabolic mechanisms that allow them to withstand, very cold temperatures.

The most obvious physical shield waterfowl use to stave off cold is a coat of insulating feathers. Feathers do not contain skin or blood vessels, and thus do not dissipate body heat. Instead, feathers actually retain body heat by trapping warm air near the skin. In addition to the flight feathers on their wings and the contour feathers covering their bodies, aquatic birds such as waterfowl possess thick layers of down, especially on their breasts and bellies. Down feathers are specialized, short fluffy plumes whose chief function is heat conservation.

Beneath the feathers is the skin, which is suffused with blood vessels that carry warm blood from inside the body to the outer surfaces. Additionally, the dermis, or layer of skin immediately below the thin outer layer of skin, is a fat-storage site. Dermal fat storage is pronounced in birds such as ducks, penguins, and loons that live in cold aquatic environments, and provides additional insulation.

Perhaps the most unique, and certainly the least apparent mechanism waterfowl employ to keep warm involves their circulatory system. Birds maintain internal body temperatures independent of outside temperatures. This is made possible because birds have separate circulatory paths from warm oxygen-rich (arterial) blood pumped from the heart, and cooler oxygen-depleted (venous) blood returning to the lungs from the body extremities.

When floating on cold water or standing on ice, their legs and feet exposed to heat-robbing loss by conduction, waterfowl and some other birds' nervous systems allow them to lessen heat loss by controlling the amount of warm arterial blood flowing into their legs, and by bypassing normal capillary circulation.

A specialized network of arteries and veins in the birds' legs accomplishes this task by acting as a heat exchanger. Constriction or dilation of these blood vessels allows the birds to retain needed body heat and to dissipate excess body heat when necessary.

In this network of arteries and veins, vessels carrying warm arterial blood pumped from the heart, and vessels carrying cold venous blood returning from the legs come in close contact. The warm blood helps elevate the temperature of the colder blood returning to the inner body. When the birds are exposed to cold temperatures, through constriction of both types of blood vessels, the amount of blood circulated through the exposed legs and feet is greatly diminished. Thus, in very cold water or air, the legs and feet can be maintained at low temperatures, creating a low heat loss gradient that helps the birds conserve energy. In fact, the body temperature of a duck or goose floating on cold water or standing on ice will remain normal (ranging from about 99 to 103 degrees F), while the temperature of its feet and legs may be only a few degrees above that of the water or surrounding air.

This Harlequin Duck has identifying metal bands on both legs. Information from such repeated bandings can provide especially valuable data to researchers.

Why are some ducks banded with man-made items?

Gaudy necklaces, oversized bracelets, body-piercing jewelry, purple "hair," and other garish body adornments aren't solely limited to punk rockers. You'll occasionally find a duck similarly appointed with these sundry trinkets and dye jobs—and looking like anything but a wild bird.

Blame waterfowl researchers for the costume designs. They've been dressing up ducks, geese, and swans since as far back as 1918, when biologists first started marking wildfowl with metal leg bands.

Today, modern researchers use several marking systems and devices to study ducks and geese. The individually numbered leg band (a kind of personal identification card), however, is still the most common tool. Bands help biologists uncover many critical factors relating to waterfowl life cycles. For example, knowing a bird's sex, its age at the time it was banded, and the time and place it is recovered by a hunter allows biologists to define survival rates and migratory paths for different species of ducks and geese.

Other devices used to identify waterfowl include plastic nasal disks and saddles (fitted over a duck's bill and held in place with a metal pin passed through the bird's nostrils); numbered, color-coded plastic neck collars and leg bands; and small metal tags pierced and locked in place through the webbing between ducklings' and goslings' toes (a painless procedure as there are few nerve endings in that area). Still other marking procedures include capturing and color-dyeing adult birds and whole broods of ducklings and goslings.

Obviously, devices such as nasal disks and saddles and neck collars, along with color-dyeing birds or attaching tiny radio transmitters to them, allow researchers to easily identify individual birds. Conspicuously marking study birds also allows biologists to obtain vital information without having to rely on the birds being shot and having their bands returned.

The unofficial waterfowl speed records are as follows—Canada goose: 20 mph ground speed, cruising speed; 60 mph airspeed, chased. Pintail: 52 mph ground speed; 65 mph airspeed, chased. Canvasback: 72 mph airspeed, chased. Redhead: 45 mph ground speed. Green-winged teal: 30 mph ground speed, cruising; 40 mph airspeed, chased.

Why do some species of ducks fly so much faster than others?

How fast do ducks really fly? Some ducks appear to be flying at speeds of 70 to 90 miles per hour, others much slower. Usually, ducks fly no faster than 40 to 60 miles per hour, although they may appear to be going much faster.

But, without a radar gun, how do we begin estimating waterfowl flight speeds? Accurately estimating waterfowl flight speeds is extremely difficult, and there are a number of factors involved.

First, let's consider ground speed versus airspeed. Airspeed is the rate at which a bird flies under its own power, without considering effects of head winds, tailwinds, or crosswinds. Ground speed is the rate at which a bird flies between two points, taking wind speeds into consideration. In other words, a bird flying at an airspeed of 30 mph with a 20 mph tailwind still has an air speed of 30 mph, but it has a ground speed of 50 mph. Flying into the same wind, it would have a ground speed of 10 mph and an airspeed of 30 mph.

It's necessary to make this distinction because most of the recordings of flight speeds of waterfowl have been made by observers from aircraft (which recorded only airspeeds), or from cars or trains pacing (ground speed) birds in flight. Some examples are included in the table below.

Thus, wind speed and direction—whether a bird is ascending and accelerating, or descending and decelerating; and whether the bird is cruising, or hitting warp speed—are variables we have to take into consideration to get an accurate clock on passing ducks and geese.

Probably more important to the waterfowl observers is understanding apparent flight speeds. Small birds appear to fly faster than larger ones, for instance, and divers appear to fly faster than dabblers because the diver's smaller wings must beat much faster to keep it aloft.

All duck species typically have large broods of anywhere from 6 to 20 ducklings.

Why do ducks raise multiple broods in some years but not others?

The truth is, with the exception of one population segment of the wood duck in North America, wild ducks do not raise more then one brood per year.

In the Upper Midwest, on the U.S. and Canadian prairies, and elsewhere above the Mason-Dixon Line, duck breeding seasons are short. Northern-nesting hens must first migrate from the South, find a nest site, lay eggs, incubate a clutch, and raise their young to flight stage in only a few months. Ducks hatched in the North may make their first autumn migration only three to six months from the day they hatch.

Double-brooding should not be confused with renesting. Renesting refers to a hen initiating a new nest after she loses her clutch, usually to a predator. If the renesting hen is successful, and this may require more than one renesting attempt if a second clutch is lost, she will still only raise one brood in a nesting season. People often observe hens with downy ducklings later in the summer and surmise that these young represent a second brood for the hen. In reality, these ducklings represent her only successful clutch.

Although most wood ducks "prefer" nesting in the North, a certain segment of their population nests in the South and leads a more leisurely lifestyle. Southern-nesting woodies are nonmigratory and don't need to semiannually accumulate huge fat reserves to feed the energy demands dictated by long journeys north and south. They also don't face the prolonged hunting pressure northern birds experience during their autumn migration. And because of favorable weather over longer periods, southern wood ducks sometimes enjoy nesting seasons as long as 140 days, which allows hens to sometimes raise two broods in a single breeding season.

Of course, as many parents, and particularly most mothers of any species might relate (if they could), raising two successive broods (of up to 15 ducklings each in the case of a wood duck hen) may not be considered a reward of a leisurely southern lifestyle. Which may be why most wood duck hens migrate north in spring after all.

This drake Mallard, like all ducks, adapted to live in the water. Their legs and feet are used primarily for propulsion in the water and are set further back on the body than those of land dwelling birds.

Why do ducks waddle when they walk?

Ducks are adapted to live most of their lives in watery environments: ponds, marshes, lakes, rivers, and oceans. Consequently, the use of their legs in water, for propulsion, is of greater consequence to them than using their legs and feet for walking on land. As a result, ducks evolved with short legs and webbed feet, and their legs and thighs are farther back on the body than those of gallinaceous birds (chickens, pheasants, turkeys, quails, etc.) that evolved to live a terrestrial lifestyle and have longer legs for greater locomotion on land.

Having its legs located farther back on its body facilitates a duck's swimming and diving abilities, even if it challenges the bird's ability to walk gracefully on *terra firma*. All ducks dive sometime or another to feed, but diving ducks and mergansers are particularly adapted to this style of food gathering, and their legs are located even farther back on their body than are the legs of dabbling ducks, which sometimes feed on land. Consequently, diving ducks are particularly clumsy when on land.

A duck's webbed feet are tremendous aids for propulsion in water. When using its legs for swimming or diving, a duck's webbed foot folds closed on the leg's forward stroke—to decrease drag—and locks open (due to the anatomical bone structure of the toes) on the backward stroke, which creates pressure against the water and propels the duck forward.

A duck uses its webbed feet in additional ways. When coming in for a landing on water, both feet are pushed out ahead of the body to make initial contact with the surface of the water and cushion the landing. In flight, especially prior to landing and just after takeoff, ducks use their webbed feet as airfoils to make minor adjustments in their flight altitude, similar to the function trim tabs play on an airplane's wings.

Duck's also are known to use their webbed feet in shallow water to disturb the bottom sediments of marshes and potholes to dislodge tiny invertebrates that live in these muddy environments. This behavior is particularly prevalent among shovelers, which sometimes join in a group effort to flush out their groceries.

The Mallard's breeding grounds are typically in the numerous lakes of the prairie provinces of Canada and northern United States. It may nest as early as February along the Pacific Coast where it is warmer. Not only do many adult hens return to previous, successful nesting areas, so too will some of their female offspring.

Why do female ducks return to nest in the same area each year?

Many female ducks return to nest in environs in which they successfully hatched and raised a brood during the previous breeding season. In the prairies and other breeding grounds of North America, not only will hens often return to the same wetland complex where they raised their previous year's ducklings, they often return to the exact pothole and may nest in the same tract of upland vegetation—sometimes in the same location, often within feet, of their previous year's nest.

To a female duck, this "homing" behavior (technically referred to as *breeding philopatry)* makes good sense. Her ability to have successfully raised a brood in an area the previous year meant that the habitat provided the essentials necessary for good duck homemaking: secure nesting cover; adequate water for pair bonding, mating, resting, bathing, and brood rearing; adequate invertebrate life to provide a protein-rich diet for the hen and her ducklings; and adequate escape cover for the hen and her ducklings to avoid predators. Not only does it make good sense to return to such an area that provides these essentials, it saves the hen valuable time and energy that would be required to explore and find a new nesting site and brood-rearing area.

Not only do adult hens return to their previous year's nesting area, so too will some of their female offspring, for the same reasons the experienced hens do. However, research has shown that older female birds (with their new mates) not only usually return to their home nesting sites earlier than their offspring, they and their mates also take up the best territories, they begin nesting earlier, and their offspring have higher survival rates. This causes the younger, less-experienced hens to take up nearby nesting sites of lesser quality or to seek out other nesting areas quite some distance away from their mother's home site.

The Common Eider breeds on the Artic coasts of Alaska and Canada and south along the coasts of Maine and Massachusetts. Hens have a better than 50% chance of returning to their prior year's nests.

Which ducks are most likely to use the same nests?

This fidelity of a hen to her previous year's successful nest site varies by species and annual habitat conditions. Ducks that nest in secure environments, such as arctic- and subarctic-nesting sea ducks, exhibit especially strong homing tendencies because their nesting habitats change little from year to year. Ducks that nest on the prairies, however, may experience changed habitat conditions from year to year as the result of wet-drought cycles, habitat loss to agricultural conversion, or other factors. And, some species of closely related dabbling ducks just do not share the same affinity for their old nesting habitats. About a third of all mallard hens exhibit homing behavior, for example, whereas only about six percent of hen blue-winged teal show an affinity to previous nesting sites. See the list below for additional examples.

Percent of Females of Various Species That Home to
Previous Breeding Area and Nest Sites

White-winged scoter	76%	Northern pintail	33%
Barrow's goldeneye	70%	Mallard	33%
Common eider	54%	Black duck	25%
Canvasback	51%	Northern shoveler	17%
American wigeon	39%	Blue-winged teal	6%

Although not as numerous as the Mallard, the graceful Northern Pintail is a widespread and common duck, with about 6 million in North America. They breed from Alaska and Labrador south to California, Nebraska, and Maine. The Pintail drake does not offer then hen a long term relationship. The real value a drake brings to the nuptials is protecting the hen from other drakes.

Why do ducks have new mates every year, while geese mate for life?

Drakes usually desert their mates once the hen begins to incubate her eggs, and drakes have nothing to do with helping to tend the brood once it hatches. By that time, the drake is long gone, either to mate with another female, or, more likely, to gather with other drakes on large bodies of water to begin their postnuptial molt.

By deserting the hen when he does, however, the drake is actually helping his mate and offspring survive. Once the hen begins incubation, she will sit on her nest almost continuously for about 28 days, leaving only for short periods to drink and eat. During this time, the drake's continued presence in the pair's territory could attract predators, which diminishes his own chances for survival and can threaten the hen and her clutch. Also, he really has no other function to perform that can benefit the hen.

The real value a drake brings to his short-term nuptial relationship is protecting the hen from other drakes. During their courtship period in spring, hens of each species are actively courted by a number of drakes. Courtship behavior is intensive and involves many undesired advances by unwanted males. Once a hen chooses a drake with which to pair and mate, however, his job is to keep other males at bay—during the pair's migration back to the nesting grounds and while the hen searches for a nest site. Once a nest site is selected, the pair will select a nearby territory—usually a small pond or portion of a marsh or pothole—which the hen and drake will occupy until the hen begins incubation. The drake's job is to defend that territory from incursions by unpaired drakes that would sexually pursue the hen.

The freedom from harassment provided by her mate allows the hen to retain energy and to spend more time feeding, which is necessary to prepare her for egg production, egg laying, and incubation. During incubation, when the hen spends most of her time on the nest, she will lose much of her stored body fat, so she must begin the nesting season in the best physical condition she possibly can.

While most diving ducks paddle with their webbed feet, the Long-tailed Duck uses its partially folded wings to propel itself underwater. One of the deepest diving ducks, it has been caught in nets as much as 200 feet below the surface.

Why do ducks dive underwater, and how deep do they go?

Ducks dive under the water for different reasons. Short, dipping dives are usually related to bathing. Ducks will also dive below the surface to avoid predators, but most often, ducks dive to forage for submerged aquatic foods.

Although all species of ducks dive on occasion, certain species dive as their primary method of feeding and are better physically adapted for obtaining aquatic food.

Diving ducks, a general classification that includes goldeneyes, canvasbacks, scaup, and redheads, as well as sea ducks such as mergansers, eiders, scoters, and long-tailed ducks (oldsquaw), have legs positioned well back on their body so they can "push" water more effectively when diving. Their wings are also not as broad or long as those of dabbling ducks (ducks that feed primarily on the surface or in very shallow water), which makes them less buoyant. Also, whereas all birds have internal air sacs connected to their lungs, the sacs of diving ducks are considerably reduced in size, which also decreases their buoyancy.

Prior to plunging below the surface, diving ducks compress their body feathers to further decrease their buoyancy, but not to the point of expelling the warm air trapped within their down feathers. All divers use their legs to propel themselves and may also use their wings to assist their forward motion.

Diving ducks' bills are also adapted to their style of feeding. The long, wedge-shaped bill of the canvasback, facilitates the bird's grubbing in bottom sediments for plant tubers. The sharp, serrated edges of mergansers' bills are ideally fashioned for capturing small fish, and the blunt, powerful bill of eiders, long-tailed ducks, and scoters are well suited for prying crustaceans, mussels and other bivalves from rocks, and then crushing the shells of these forage items.

Most of the time, divers only have to reach moderate depths to find food, and they remain underwater for only short periods. When necessary, however, they will dive much deeper. The depth-record-holder is the long-tailed duck, which has been known to forage in ocean water depths as great as 240 feet.

The Wood Duck is the only native North American duck that
both nests in tree cavities and perches in tree branches.

Why don't ducks perch in trees like other birds do?

Actually, some do. There is an entire taxonomical division of waterfowl known as *Carinini,* or perching ducks. Of the 13 recognized species of these ducks, however, only one, the wood duck, occurs naturally in North America. Another species, the mandarin duck, has been introduced to California, where a small breeding population of this brilliantly colored duck exists.

The wood duck, like most perching ducks, inhabits wooded areas and nests in tree cavities in or near forested wetlands. Both the adults and the young have sharply clawed toes, which help them grasp tree branches when perching and climbing in and out of nest cavities.

Like most perching ducks, wood ducks live in shaded, forested terrain, and have relatively large eyes to help them dwell in this type of low-light habitat. Another adaptation they exhibit is a relatively long, broad tail, which increases their agility in flight and helps them to maneuver quickly when flying amidst closely spaced trees.

Wood ducks, however, are not the only waterfowl in North America that sometimes roost in trees. The fulvous whistling duck and black-bellied whistling duck—both found on the Gulf Coast—are sometimes called "tree ducks." These species do sometimes perch in trees—especially the black-bellied whistling duck, which also nests in tree cavities—but, taxonomically, they are not true perching ducks. To learn more about these curious birds, see page 73.

Still other North American ducks are known to nest in tree cavities, but are not otherwise known to perch on tree limbs and branches. These include a few species of sub-Arctic-nesting sea ducks, including the bufflehead, common goldeneye, Barrow's goldeneye, and some merganser species. Some hens of these species utilize tree cavities that are excavated by woodpeckers, especially flickers, and may return to nest in the same cavity in successive breeding seasons. In areas where the breeding range of some of these arboreal-nesting ducks overlap, competition for available tree cavities is often fierce, and females may destroy the eggs of other hens when usurping a nest cavity for their own use.

Breeding from Alaska south and east to Nebraska and Minnesota, Canvasbacks migrate to large prairie marshes during the summer, and spend the winter on large lakes, bays, and estuaries.

Why do ducks migrate?

Migration for ducks is a biological necessity. Their fall migration to southern wintering areas is prompted by climatic conditions on their breeding grounds, where freezing temperatures bring ice and snow. Consequently, the birds simply could not survive if they did not migrate.

On their wintering grounds, ducks become more widely dispersed because natural food resources are relatively limited and spread over larger geographic areas. Also, some duck species—wood ducks, mottled ducks, and mallards, particularly—that reside year round in the southern wintering grounds fully exploit these areas' best habitats, including their food sources. Where natural foods such as mast, plant seeds and tubers, invertebrates, and other such items are lacking, wintering ducks may feed in agricultural fields, eating waste grains of wheat, corn, rice, and soybeans. Over the winter months, though, as food resources are consumed and become limited, food shortages become one of the motivating factors for ducks to begin their migration north.

Ducks will generally begin their spring migration by following the thaw line as it progresses ever northward. On their journey north, ducks will feed on waste grains, on naturally occurring perennial plant seeds, and on invertebrate life that begins proliferating in abundance in shallow, temporary potholes.

Finding food and conserving energy during the spring migration are imperative to ducks, especially hens. For them to be able to produce eggs and reproduce, they must maintain adequate fat and protein reserves in their bodies. Some of that fat and protein may be gained on the wintering grounds, but it must be preserved as body "stores" for successful reproduction, and more fat and protein must be gathered on the journey home to the breeding grounds.

When ducks do return to the breeding areas and hatch their young, the long days of sunlight and warmth produce an almost unlimited profusion of plant and animal foods that sustain the adult birds and allow the many hatchlings of the various species to grow to adult size and fledge within a few short months.

At night, ducks are known to navigate through celestial observation of the moon and stars.

Why do ducks migrate at night?

Ducks (and other migratory birds) migrate at all hours of the day and night. Depending on whether they are flying in daylight or dark, however, they employ any of a number of navigational tools that help to keep them on course.

Ducks often fly traditional routes defined by visual landmarks. The landmarks can be coasts of oceans or large lakes (such as the Great Lakes), mountain fronts, or river valleys. Other visual clues include the sun's position and even polarized light, which somehow allows the birds to perform some sort of compass navigation. At night, ducks are known to navigate through celestial observation of the moon and stars, suggesting that the birds follow a form of stellar map.

Radar studies of nighttime migrations have also determined that ducks will continue on course even when they are flying between dense layers of clouds that prohibit the birds from seeing the stars or landmarks. Researchers have long believed that in situations like this, birds navigate by an unknown form of orientation to the earth's magnetic field.

The migration routes that ducks follow in fall are to some degree learned by each new generation of ducks. By flying south with migration-experienced adults of their own species, the juvenile birds are thought to be able to learn their species' traditional navigational landmarks and migrational resting stops.

Still other research suggests that ducks may have some innate sense of their species' traditional migration paths. Researchers have captured young ducklings of wild ducks and held the juvenile birds in captivity until all others of their species had migrated south for the winter. When these young ducks were banded and later released, band recoveries indicated that the birds migrated along the same path of the adults, but without the guidance of the older birds and without any prior knowledge of navigational landmarks.

Do ducks still get lost in the dark? Yes. Under extremely poor light conditions and overcast skies at night, flocks of ducks have been known to land on lighted football fields and shopping mall parking lots.

These Northern Shovelers are in a loose V formation, with the ducks in back drafting the ones in front.

Why do ducks fly in V formation?

Ducks do not always fly in V formation, and when they do, certain species (canvasbacks and mallards, for example) show a greater tendency to fly in this type of formation than others do.

When ducks are in groups and making relatively short flights across a marshland or from water to nearby agricultural fields to feed, they generally fly at low altitudes and in amorphous bunches.

In fall, however, when larger groups of ducks of the same species assemble to migrate, they fly at much higher altitudes, from 500 to 5,000 feet. Flock sizes vary, but most groups contain 25 to 50 birds. These flocks may be strung out in a line forming a blunt arc or, less often, a sharp-pointed V. Sometimes groups will appear as a formless, gyrating bunch of birds that will shift into a V or J-shaped formation, maintain that formation for a period, then disassemble in a shapeless group once more.

When ducks are flying in V formation they do so for two reasons: (1) to save energy and (2) to maintain visual contact with other members in the flock.

When a bird flies, it pushes the air directly in front of it, forming a small high-pressure area. In its path, directly behind the bird, is an area of lower-pressure. It is by flying behind and slightly to the side of the bird ahead of it—in the "still" air behind the leading duck—that a following duck can avoid fighting high-pressure and thus save energy. Just like race car drivers closely follow a leading car, "drafting" the vehicle ahead of it and avoiding the slipstream of rough air produced by its movement, ducks draft one another in formation.

But a duck doesn't fly directly behind the bird in front of it. If it did, it would lose sight of the birds behind it. Also, ducks don't fly in a straight line, wing to wing, or they wouldn't save energy and wouldn't have a leader to follow. Instead, the birds compromise some energy savings to maintain visual communication by flying slightly to the side of the bird ahead of it. The lead-bird position in a migrating flock is periodically swapped between members of the flock to keep flock leaders from becoming overly fatigued.

The smallest of the mergansers, Hoodeds are most often seen along rivers and in estuaries during the fall and winter.

Why do some ducks migrate later than others?

Authorities on waterfowl migration correlate changes in the physical environment with the initiation of migration. Among these are temperature, barometric pressure, and changes in the day-length cycle (photoperiod). The actual causes of migration are probably a combination of all or some of these factors.

The degree to which any of these factors affects a particular species differs. Blue-winged teal or canvasback begin to depart from their breeding areas in fall on about the same date each year, regardless of weather, while mallards, may or may not begin migration until freeze-up occurs and food availability is gone. So, some segments of the mallard population are moving south in early October, while others may not begin migrating until December.

Although most ducks fly directly from their breeding grounds to their wintering areas along relatively well-defined flyways, this is not always the case with all ducks. Some birds move out of the breeding grounds to inhabit new areas, prior to migration, in late summer or early fall.

During this time, especially mid- to late summer, most adult waterfowl go through a flightless period during which they molt their flight feathers. This time of flightlessness may be spent in an area entirely different and up to hundreds of miles away from their breeding grounds. When their new flight feathers are grown, the birds begin migrating south again. This type of movement is predominantly seen in canvasbacks and redheads, and especially in males of these species. Juveniles may stay on the breeding grounds or wander to new areas many miles from their natal wetlands prior to migrating.

There is considerable complexity in the migration of duck species as there is a difference in the timing of migration between males and females as well as adults and juveniles of the same species.

Generally speaking, males are on the wing before females and juveniles. This is especially evident in such birds as later-migrating female and juvenile lesser scaup. In fact, many adult males of some species of ducks may migrate through the northern tier of states before autumn weather arrives.

This flock consists of Long-tailed Ducks and one Bufflehead. The Long-tailed Duck, formerly known as the Oldsquaw, breeds in Alaska and Artic Canada and winters along coasts from the Bering Sea south to California, from Labrador south to the Carolinas, along portions of the Gulf Coast, and on the Great Lakes.

Why do ducks fly so high when they migrate? Wouldn't it require less energy to fly closer to the ground?

How high waterfowl fly when migrating is a function of the season, the distance to be flown, wind conditions, and the terrain over which the birds are flying.

Over water, ducks such as oldsquaws (now for the purpose of political correctness called long-tailed ducks) and scoters may make migration flights at altitudes varying from only a few feet to 1,000 feet above the water. Over land, however, the same ducks' flight altitudes may average above 3,000 feet, ranging from 500 to 5,000 feet, often depending on favorable winds at varying altitudes. Flying higher, and finding a good tail-wind, saves ducks more energy than required for them to reach the greater altitude.

Snow geese, which commonly make very long nonstop fall migration flights, are high-altitude specialists. Flocks of these geese have been reported by airplane pilots at extreme altitudes of up to 20,000 feet. Canada geese, which make much shorter fall migrations, usually migrate at much lower altitudes, averaging about 2,500 feet above the ground.

In spring, when migrations for both ducks and geese are usually punctuated by a series of shorter flights and take place over a longer period, flight altitudes are lower than those of fall migrations. During spring migration, geese commonly fly in large flocks as they do in their fall migrations. Ducks, by contrast, will migrate north as pairs, in small groups of unmated adult ducks, or in larger groups of juvenile ducks such as some diver and sea duck species that don't reach sexual maturity until their second or third year of life.

Although waterfowl will migrate by day or night, most flights begin at dusk and end by dawn. As dusk approaches, and at a signal known only to the birds themselves, they lift off together and head skyward as a group.

Why do ducks make mass migrations?

It is a rare event when wide-scale brutal cold and harsh north winds drive masses of ducks of all species from the North simultaneously. Such a mass movement of ducks (and geese), referred to as a "grand passage," is a sight not easily forgotten by those fortunate enough to witness one. Wave after wave of ducks and geese will pass overhead, and in some recorded instances, more than 200,000 waterfowl have been witnessed flying over a single large marsh during such a grand passage.

By meteorological necessity, mass migrations may be initiated at any time of the day. However, seemingly by choice, and although waterfowl will migrate by day or night, most migratory flights begin at dusk and end by dawn. Such flights are usually made by geese as cohesive units that stay assembled for the entirety of the migratory voyage. Individual ducks or newly forming breeding pairs of ducks, however, commonly change flock membership over the course of migrating.

Prior to initiating a migratory departure, ducks will begin flocking as dusk approaches. The gathering birds will become increasingly active as they assemble: preening, wing flapping, calling to one another. As darkness approaches, and at a signal known only to the birds themselves, they will lift off together and head skyward as a group, usually departing in the direction they will follow throughout the night (or day).

The departure of one flock of ducks (or geese) often stimulates, along with the harsh weather, other flocks to take wing too, and these separate but associated flocks may form "chains" that communicate through interflock calling throughout the flight. The calling not only helps keep different flocks in touch with one another but also helps space out individuals within the flocks, thus avoiding midair collisions in darkness or in clouds and fog.

Once airborne and having attained the desired altitude, ducks will adjust their flying speed according to the speed of the wind, be it a headwind or tailwind, to keep their ground speed fairly constant.

Mallards are agile fliers who can take off almost vertically.

Why do some ducks leap out of the water and begin flying, while others have to take a running/flapping start to become airborne?

The ability (or inability) to take flight from a floating position on water or a standing position on land is a function of a duck's anatomy. A duck's anatomy, in turn, is the result of its genetics and ecological pressures mandating certain adaptations to the environment.

For example, species such as mallards, teal, pintails, and other dabbling ducks that frequent small bodies of water such as ponds and potholes require a way to quickly escape predators that could stalk close to the water's edge. Consequently, dabblers evolved with long, broad wings (relative to their body size) that could lift them off the water almost vertically, much like a helicopter takes to the air.

Sea ducks and other diving ducks, by contrast, inhabit large bodies of water where they are much safer from predators, and where they obtain food by diving for mollusks and submergent vegetation. Many diving ducks utilize their wings in addition to their feet to propel them underwater. In this case, large, broad wings would create resistance against the water and hinder a duck's movement. Consequently, diving ducks evolved shorter, narrower wings relative to their body size.

For diving ducks, however, improved mobility under the water is a trade-off with the lifting capacity larger wings provide. As a result, divers have to taxi into the wind (like a floatplane instead of a helicopter), flapping their wings and paddling their feet across the water, building up speed until aerodynamics allow them to take off. Once airborne, the smaller wings of divers also require them to beat their wings at a faster rate—as opposed to equivalent-size dabbling ducks—to remain aloft.

Head bobbing allows this Blue-winged Teal to double and triple check distances between itself and the other objects in its immediate environment.

Why do ducks pump their heads up and down prior to taking flight?

Ducks must turn their head and neck to change the direction of their vision because their eyes are essentially fixed in their sockets and can only be moved to a very limited degree, and because their eyes are located on either side of their head, providing the birds very little ability to judge distances. In humans, with our relatively close-set eyes positioned on the front of our head, we can optically triangulate an object when we view it, allowing us to determine its distance quite accurately.

Consequently, given their limited perception of depth and distance, when ducks prepare to take flight, they will "bob" their head, giving them a quick succession of rapidly changing views of an object (including other ducks around them, approaching predators, etc.) at slightly different angles, which allows a duck to better estimate the distance between itself, other ducks, approaching predators, the shoreline, or anything else in its immediate environment.

But head bobbing also serves other important functions. It synchronizes the ducks' movement as a flock (or as a pair), and additionally serves to alert other ducks in the flock of the possible approach of danger. Whatever the case, one bird in a flock will begin head bobbing to alert the rest of the flock that it is time to fly away from the immediate location. Other ducks will see the head-bobbing behavior and emulate it until each bird in the flock is bobbing its head and has oriented its body head-first into the wind, at which point the flock will take off simultaneously.

This type of behavior has obvious advantages when it comes to survival, and it is one reason why ducks assemble in flocks outside of the breeding season. First, with many eyes on the lookout, there is a greater chance that one or more ducks will recognize the threat of an approaching eagle, fox, coyote, or other predator. Second, by signaling all the ducks in the flock to take off at the same time, there is less of a chance of leaving behind stragglers, which are often picked off by swift, skillful predators.

The Wood Duck is an early spring migrant. It arrives at the northern part of its breeding range in March-April after ice has left woodland ponds and wetlands. In the fall, it moves south from October through December.

Why do ducks fly in rain, sleet, and snow? Aren't they blinded by the weather?

No. Like other birds, cats, frogs, and many other vertebrates, ducks possess a third, thin eyelid that protects their eyes from the sting of raindrops, sleet, and snow. As well as fleshy, opaque upper and lower eyelids, ducks have a third lid that underlies these outer lids. The third lid is a single transparent membrane that is normally retracted in the corner of the eye near the bill but can be pulled back over the eye, posteriorly, to cover and clean the cornea. This third eyelid is called a *nictitating membrane,* from the verb nictitate, which means "wink."

It is interesting to note that while ducks have outer eyelids similar to those of humans, the outer eyelids of ducks are used to close the birds' eyes only when they sleep, while the nictitating membrane is used to blink. The inside surface of the nictitating membrane, also referred to as the nictitans, is covered with brush-shaped cells that brush the cornea with tears when the lid is blinked.

In flight during unfavorable weather, ducks can draw their nictitans over their eyes for protection, much like a pilot of an open-cockpit aircraft would wear goggles to protect his eyes. Not only are the membranes transparent, allowing the birds to see when flying with their nictitans covering their corneas, they are also optically clear enough to allow the birds to fly without distorting their vision and causing them to become disoriented.

The nictitating membrane serves an additional purpose for ducks that dive underwater to obtain food. When submerged, ducks cover their eyes with the nictitans to shield their corneas and to provide lens-like correction to their vision to overcome the magnifying effect of water. In this instance, the nictitating membranes serve the birds much like a pair of underwater contact lenses.

The nictitating membranes are obviously important to ducks, but the membranes are vulnerable to parasitic infestation (rare occurrences) and also subject to paralysis in birds infected with avian botulism.

The tall, long-legged Black-bellied Whistling Duck is known for emitting
loud, shrill whistling calls—hence its nickname "Squeaker."

Why do some ducks whistle and squeal instead of quack?

Certain long, slender ducks found in and near the Gulf Coast states are known locally as "squealers." These two species of ducks, whose official common names are the black-bellied whistling duck and the fulvous whistling duck, are strange ducks indeed. In many ways, they share more biological traits with geese than they do other ducks.

Both of these species of whistling ducks (there are nine total worldwide) are more commonly found in Mexico and Latin America, where they are called *pichichi, pijia,* or *pato maizal.* Like their other whistling duck cousins across the globe, the black-bellied and fulvous whistling ducks are known for emitting loud, shrill whistling calls, especially in flight. And while many whistling ducks perch in trees, they should not be confused with true perching ducks that also emit high-pitched squealing vocalizations, such as the female wood duck.

As mentioned, although taxonomically classified as ducks, in many respects whistling ducks more closely resemble geese and swans in behavior and appearance. For instance, male and female whistling ducks show no sexual dimorphism (outward difference in sexual characteristics). Both sexes share, as do geese and swans, almost identical plumage color and patterns. Whistling ducks also molt that similar plumage only once per year, as do geese and swans, whereas other ducks molt twice each year. Whistling ducks share other characteristics common to geese and swans. Among them are long legs, long necks, an erect stance, and the absence of a typical duck-like waddle when they walk.

When it comes to certain behaviors, whistling ducks also act more like geese and swans than other duck species. Like geese and swans, whistling ducks form lifelong pair bonds instead of finding new mates each year. This leads to another behavior common to geese and swans but not shared with other ducks: male whistling ducks share egg incubation duties with their female mates. Once the young are hatched, both whistling duck parents also escort their brood and remain with the young until months after the young reach flight stage.

The Harlequin is a bird of freshwater mountain streams during the breeding season, but in the fall, the birds move to the coast where they dive for crabs, mussels, and other crustaceans in the ocean.

Why do some ducks live in saltwater environments, while other species prefer freshwater habitats?

Ducks are found in a variety of watery environments, including saltwater, brackish water, and freshwater. Some sea ducks spend most of their life cycles in coastal or deep sea saltwater habitats but prefer to breed and raise their young inland, near freshwater marshes and ponds. Other sea ducks lead almost an exclusively marine lifestyle, rarely leaving saltwater during their lifetimes. Still other species of dabbling and diving ducks may spend equal amounts of time in saltwater and freshwater habitats.

As ducks evolved and adapted to specialized habitat niches, they became specialized in, among other characteristics, what types of areas they chose for nest sites and the types of foods they ate. Those birds that became particularly adapted to brackish and saltwater habitats developed large supraorbital salt glands (located inside the head and above the orbit of the eye), which filter the blood of excess salt and excrete it as a highly concentrated saline solution through the birds' nostrils. These salt-excreting organs are especially well developed (to a degree that they may modify the head profile) in species such as eiders, scoters, and long-tailed ducks, which feed primarily on marine plant and animal organisms high in salt content (bivalves such as clams and mussels as well as marine worms and crustaceans), and also ingest considerable amounts of saltwater when feeding.

Other ducks that nest in freshwater marshes may winter almost entirely in marine environments. Almost the entire continental population of redhead ducks, for instance, winters in the highly saline Laguna Madre on the Gulf Coast. Black ducks that nest on inland beaver ponds and freshwater lakes and marshes often winter in brackish coastal marshes of the Atlantic Seaboard. Species such as these, as well as the majority of ducks, geese, and swans, have functional but not highly developed salt glands, however, and must travel at least once or twice daily to inland freshwater sources to drink.

Waterfowl possess innate navigational abilities allowing them to follow celestial cues,
to wind direction, turbulence patterns, and possibly to the earth's magnetic field.

Why don't ducks get lost when they fly at night, in clouds, or out of sight of land?

We know that migrating ducks stay on their traditional flight paths by following geographical landmarks (large rivers, mountain ranges, ocean and lake shorelines) during daylight hours and while flying in good weather. Scientist believe ducks and other migratory birds also utilize other visual navigational clues, including the sun's azimuth and altitude, polarized light, and, at night, star configurations.

Yet we also know that waterfowl migrate during cloudy conditions, sometimes between or over cloud layers that render visible landmarks or celestial cues ineffective. Rader observations show that the birds still stay on course. Obviously, waterfowl have means other to help them stay within their migration corridors.

A great deal of research on migrating bird species, including waterfowl, indicates that birds possess innate navigation abilities that allow them to utilize other navigational information when flying out of sight of land over vast expanses of water. These capabilities allow the birds to orient themselves according to the aforementioned celestial cues, to wind direction and turbulence patterns, and possibly to the earth's magnetic field.

Scientists believe that young waterfowl learn migration routes by accompanying older birds on their semiannual passages. This is certainly true for geese and cranes, which migrate as family units to and from the breeding and wintering areas. Ducks no doubt learn migration routes from experience too, but they may also possess a form of genetic memory, an inherited, built-in road map that assists them in locating wintering areas and, especially in the case of female ducks, to return in spring to their natal marshes. Dr. Frank Bellrose conducted studies with young-of-the-year blue-winged teal that had been captured and not released until all older teal had migrated from the capture site. Remarkably, with no older ducks to lead the way, the young bluewings migrated on their own, and followed the same direction taken by the older birds to their wintering area. Similar experiments with other species have yielded similar results.

This image shows the inner speculum feathers of the drake Mallard, which are metallic purplish blue bordered in front and back with white.

Why do ducks molt their feathers and become flightless? How can they migrate without flight feathers?

Feathers, regardless of how well a duck preens and cares for them, eventually wear out and require replacing. As a general rule, all waterfowl replace each of their feathers every year and become flightless, but only for a short period of time outside of the migration period. Swans, geese, and whistling ducks molt only once per year, but most ducks undergo two molts per year.

Unlike songbirds and gallinaceous birds (turkeys, grouse, chickens), which molt their flight feathers sequentially and never become flightless, waterfowl lose their flight feathers simultaneously during the summer molt and remain flightless for a period ranging from three weeks (small ducks such as teal) to five to six weeks (geese and swans). In ducks, body feathers are replaced twice a year, but flight feathers are only shed during the summer molt.

Drakes usually undergo the summer molt shortly after they leave their mates, when the hens begin incubating their eggs. Unpaired drakes molt at about the same time, generally beginning in June or July.

During their flightless period, the brightly colored drakes' breeding plumage is replaced with an inconspicuous drab brown "eclipse" plumage that resembles the plain, dowdy plumage of the females, which helps to camouflage them.

Female ducks do not begin the summer molt until after their young are hatched and she begins brood rearing. Consequently, both she and her offspring are flightless and vulnerable for a time until she grows new flight feathers and her young grow their first adult plumage and fledge. During that time, the hens will seek wetlands that provide adequate food and dense cover for concealment from predators. More often than not, the hen will still be flightless as her young reach flight stage and depart for other areas.

When ducks replace their flight feathers, they are able to fly again in late summer or early autumn. Although their flight feathers have been replaced, the remainder of their eclipse plumage body feathers will molt and be replaced over the next few months.

A group of hen Mallards resting on a log.

Why are drake mallards so rarely seen in the Gulf Coast states, while hens are so prevalent and often seen as pairs?

Mallards winter along the Gulf of Mexico, but not in large numbers. Consequently, some migratory green-headed drake mallards may be seen in Florida, Alabama, Mississippi, Louisiana, and Texas during November through March. Relatively small numbers of resident breeding mallards are also found in all of these states throughout the year, but the drakes are not conspicuous in the summer months when they are in their eclipse plumage.

The hen mallards that seem so prevalent in southern Florida and the Gulf Coast are actually mottled ducks, which are a separate subspecies of the mallard in which the males and females share a drab brown plumage that closely resembles that of the hen mallard.

The mottled duck of the Florida peninsula, the Florida mottled duck, is confined to the southern portion of the state but found as far north as Tampa. The shorter-necked Gulf mottled duck is found in coastal lowlands on the Gulf of Mexico, from Alabama west and south to Mexico.

Although both the Florida and Gulf mottled duck of both sexes resemble female mallards, they have longer necks and tend to be darker in color, but with pale brown to buff-colored heads. The Florida drake has a bright yellow bill, the Gulf drake an olive green bill. The females of both mottled ducks have orange bills with dark spots.

Yet another close relative of the mallard is the Mexican duck, a subspecies that resembles mottled ducks in coloration but is confined to the Rio Grande and Pecos river valleys in New Mexico, Arizona, and west Texas.

Both sexes of yet another close relative of the mallard, the American black duck, share plumages that resemble the hen mallard, but are much darker. Black ducks nest across eastern North America but may winter as far south as Louisiana. Because of their much darker plumage and white underwings, they are rarely confused with resident mottled ducks during the winter period along the Gulf Coast.

Many Wood Ducks court and pair in fall and winter when most are on inland waters of the southern United States. While hens tend their nests, drakes congregate in flocks prior to making their molt migration.

When male ducks desert their mates when the hens begin to incubate, where do they go and what do they do?

When a drake deserts his mate, he may stay in the general area and try to find other hens with which to mate. Otherwise, he will eventually leave the breeding area and undergo a molt migration. In leaving the nesting hen, the drake not only is less likely to attract predators to her and her clutch, he is also forsaking the breeding grounds and its food sources, which the hen will need for energy to replace her feathers when she molts and that the ducklings will need for growth. Hens will usually molt in the same area where they raised their brood.

Drakes of numerous duck (and goose) species, especially those that nest in the prairies or Upper Midwest, often congregate in flocks prior to making their molt migration. The flocks are composed of males of a particular species that have bred that spring as well as the more numerous nonbreeding drakes that failed to find mates, or in the case of some species, males that do not reach sexual maturity until their second and sometimes third year of life.

Molt migration routes are usually northward from the breeding areas, and are often quite distant, sometimes up to more than a thousand miles from where the abandoned hens are nesting. The goal of ducks undertaking a molt migration is to find large bodies of water with abundant food where they can undergo their summer molt and flightless period in relative safety. Abundant food is necessary because feathers are composed almost entirely of protein, and for the birds to grow a new set of feathers requires that they eat large quantities of protein-rich foods such as aquatic invertebrates and good quality wetland vegetation.

Some places are traditional molting areas for certain species of ducks. For instance, thousands of drake mallards gather at Delta Marsh, Manitoba, every summer to molt. Molting pintail drakes congregate on large marshes in Idaho and lakes north of Regina, Saskatchewan, as well as traveling much farther north to molt on the Mackenzie River Delta in the Northwest Territories.

Mallards lay 8-10 light olive-green eggs in a down-lined nest often placed some distance from water, and occasionally even in a tree. The egg mass of a completed clutch can comprise half the weight of the hen.

Why do ducks lay such large eggs?

Proportionate to a laying hen's mass and body size, the eggs of ducks are quite large compared to eggs laid by most other bird species. Ducks' clutches are also larger, usually from six to 12 eggs per clutch, than those of many birds, especially clutches of songbirds, shorebirds, gulls, terns, which may lay only from two to four eggs. Often, a completed clutch of duck eggs may weigh from 20 to 30 percent of the body weight of the laying female. For mallards, the egg mass of a completed clutch often weighs half of what the hen weighs. And the hen ruddy duck, which takes the prize for laying some of the largest eggs of all ducks, commonly produces a clutch that may exceed her own weight.

Duck eggs need to be large. They are packages containing all the elements that will make up a hatchling's bone, fiber, tissue, and a layer of soft downy feathers. Ducks hatch ready to leave the nest in a few short hours and are able to walk and feed themselves. To assure they have the ability to do so, the egg must be large enough to contain all the building blocks required for this type of advanced development (as compared to songbirds, for example, that stay in the nest for days after hatching and are fed by their parents). And, the larger the egg, the longer it will take the hen to incubate it and bring the contained embryo to full development. Ducks usually incubate their eggs over a period of approximately four weeks, compared to the two-week incubation period of most songbirds.

Producing and incubating so many large eggs places a great nutritional demand on hens. According to biologist Holly Dickson, "When and where hens get the [nutritional] resources needed to produce eggs varies by species. For most ducks, there are two sources: (1) the habitats where they have spent the winter and migrated through before they get to the breeding grounds, and (2) the wetlands on which the hen actually chooses to nest. Large ducks tend to bring [stored as body fat, etc.] most of the resources with them to the breeding area, especially if they are early nesters like mallards and pintail. Later-nesting ducks [teal, wigeon, etc. have much more time to extract needed nutrients directly from the breeding area. Smaller-bodied ducks such as teal cannot carry large amounts of fat during migration and must seek energy sources after arriving on the nesting area. For these ducks, nesting is delayed until there is enough food available to support egg production and incubation."

Once hens begin incubation, they spend increasing amounts of time on their nests and less time feeding. And beginning with egg laying and continuing over the four-weeks of incubation, a hen mallard can burn up as much as 60 percent of her stored body reserves.

The Black-bellied Whistling Duck is unique in that both sexes are similar in appearance, and the male stays with the female through brood rearing.

A Northern Pintail Duck courtship flock. Male Northern Pintails are aggressive, often forcing their attentions on females of other species.

Why are roving groups of male ducks so prevalent in spring?

They are on the prowl, looking for hens with which to mate. And sometimes, as a group, they behave like a gang of overzealous teenage suitors (or gang members).

According to Michael Furtman, in his book *Duck Country,* "Ducks usually court in groups, a behavior called social courtship that likely evolved because males outnumber females [in wild duck populations], and so must compete for selection. To this end, drake ducks developed displays and plumage that are intended to be attractive and gain a hen's attention. During the courting season, the marshes have all the hormonal tension of a high school hallway, and are nearly as noisy as well. Unpaired hens call brashly to attract mates, and drakes strut about emitting weird guttural gruntings, wheezings… all while adopting strange postures, kicking up water, and picking fights."

And the drakes like to chase the girls. Courtship rituals sometimes involve group flights in which many males pursue a single unpaired hen. Large courtship flights (a dozen or more males chasing a single hen) are especially prominent in certain species such as blue-winged teal, American widgeon, and northern pintail.

More often, a group of drakes will vie for the attention of a single unpaired hen by performing physical and vocal displays. Furtman says, "The displays are quite similar among most Northern Hemisphere dabbling ducks, and at various times can be directed at the hen, directed at rival drakes, or directed simultaneously toward both. In any case, to be successful a drake must first attract a hen's attention and intimidate his rivals. In this melee of group sexual tension, each drake tries to direst his displaying efforts toward the hen, and each attempts to position himself near her. As you might imagine, with all this testosterone flowing, competition is fierce and fights commonly erupt. Drakes sometimes tear into each other with the savagery of a cockfight."

All of this behavior points to the advantage of a hen pairing quickly with a dominant drake that can defend her from the advances of prowling, amorous males.

Unlike other dabbling ducks that form pairs in the fall, the Blue-winged Teal begins courting in the spring and often does not acquire the familiar breeding plumage until December or January. When preening, ducks like this Blue-winged Teal appear to pay close attention to their tail feathers. Actually, they are oiling their plumage, bills and legs.

Why do ducks preen their tail feathers?

When preening, ducks appear to give an unusual amount of attention to their tail feathers. Actually, however, ducks preen all of their feathers, including their tail feathers, for a number of reasons, including cleaning, parasite removal, and feather maintenance. Some preening behavior, on the other hand, has nothing to do with tidiness.

As in all birds, a duck feather is made up of a central shaft, on either side of which extend a series of interlocking barbs and barbules (somewhat like a zipper). These barbs and barbules often become unlocked (unzipped) and must be restored to their proper form in order to stay flight worthy and to help maintain their water resistance. To relock the interlocking parts of a feather, a duck firmly and slowly draws the feather's shaft between the upper and lower portions of its bill, prompting the barbs and barbules to interlock once more.

When doing maintenance preening, ducks especially appear to pay more attention to their tail feathers. Actually, what they are doing is oiling their plumage, bills, and legs. At the posterior extremity of a duck's body is a fleshy and bony prominence called a *uropygium* (but more commonly and irreverently referred to as a "pope's nose") that supports the tail feathers. The uropygium also contain's an oil-producing gland (uropygial gland) that opens near the base of the tail feathers. Ducks use their bill to take this oil and repeatedly spread it over their entire plumage in order to waterproof it, and to preserve the surface condition of their legs and bill.

Not all preening is performed in order to clean or maintain feather integrity; some of this behavior can be social in nature. Both paired and unpaired ducks have been observed engaging in mutual preening, or "nibbling." Mutual preening between mated ducks is especially prevalent in wood duck pairs. Other preening movements function as sexual displays during courtship and mating, and as threat displays toward other ducks.

The Red-breasted Merganser lives mainly on fish, which it captures in swift underwater dives, aided by its long pointed bill lined with sharp, tooth-like projections.

Why do some ducks have pointy bills like chickens' beaks?

Mergansers have long, slender bills that they use for catching fish. Other than these "fish ducks," there really are no species of ducks that have pointy beaks like a chicken's. There are, however, three species of waterbirds that are commonly mistaken for ducks and have chicken-like beaks.

The first and most common of these waterbirds is the American coot. Both sexes in coot share the same bluish black plumage color and have a buff to whitish pointed beak. Coots commonly swim about in the open, as do ducks, but also walk about on shore and on mats of floating vegetation in wetlands. The birds have strong legs and large feet with three long, lobed toes. Coots eat mostly vegetation but will consume just about anything they can find in a wetland habitat, including insects, fish, worms, snails, and crayfish. They consume these items by foraging along the water surface, grazing on land, and diving underwater. Coots are accomplished divers. Their large, lobed feet act like paddles and help propel them both on and underwater.

The second-most common waterbird commonly mistaken for a duck is the common moorhen. Moorhen resemble coots but are found mostly in the eastern half of the United States, and most often east of the Mississippi River. Bluish black except for some white in their tail and a buff to white beak tip and a prominent bright red upper beak, moorhens swim buoyantly, bobbing their head as they do so, and walk and run on land and through thick marsh vegetation. This bird is often found in the company of coots and ducks on freshwater marshes that have considerable plant growth.

Another bird mistaken for a true duck is the purple gallinule. The gallinule, or "swamp hen," resembles a coot in size and body form, but is much more colorful than a coot. The purple gallinule shows an emerald green hue across its back and has an iridescent purple cast to the plumage along its neck, breast, and belly. A gallinule has long legs with long, slender toes that allow it to walk on floating lily pads and through marsh vegetation.

A Northern Pintail and Mallard flock. Some migration corridors follow distinct landscape features including mountain ranges. Next page: Mallards tipping up.

Why do ducks migrate along the same flight paths each year? Do they know where they're going?

Yes, ducks know where they're going—north in spring, south in winter. But that statement oversimplifies a series of complex events and it's not always correct—some waterfowl migrate east to west (eiders, harlequins, some segments of dabbling and diving duck populations), some don't migrate at all (Florida and Gulf Coast mottled ducks and southern resident wood ducks), and segments of some duck and goose populations (mallards especially, as well as certain populations of Canada geese) migrate in some years but not in others. There are, in fact, myriad fascinating aspects to waterfowl migrations (the mythical belief that hummingbirds migrate south on the backs of geese is not one of them).

But, do ducks know where they are going when they migrate? Radar observations of ducks in flight indicate that migrating flocks will adjust their direction if they encounter crosswinds, suggesting that the birds correct their course to stay on a predetermined flight path. Staying on a flight path implies that migrating waterfowl have a concept of where they are and where they want to go. Indeed, Dr. Frank Bellrose and other biologists—using radar observations and aircraft to follow migrating waterfowl, and analyzing duck band returns and other data—have established that waterfowl migrate inside well-defined traditional corridors on their trips to their wintering areas.

Investigators have further determined that some mallards consistently use 50- to 150-mile-wide migration corridors; in other instances, corridors may be as narrow as 10 miles wide. Inside these corridors, according to Bellrose, "…nocturnally migrating waterfowl will cover a broad front, with little suggestion that routes, per se, are being followed… The migration corridors …represent passageways, each connecting a series of waterfowl habitats extending from the breeding grounds to the wintering grounds." It should come as no surprise, then, that some migration corridors follow natural landscape features such as large rivers, mountain ranges, and ocean and Great Lakes shorelines.